Angel Sharks

by Grace Hansen

abdopublishing.com

Published by Abdo Kids, a division of ABDO, PO Box 398166, Minneapolis, Minnesota 55439.

Printed in the United States of America, North Mankato, Minnesota.

102016

012016

 THIS BOOK CONTAINS RECYCLED MATERIALS

Photo Credits: Alamy, AP Images, Corbis, iStock, Minden Pictures, Science Source, Thinkstock

Production Contributors: Teddy Borth, Jennie Forsberg, Grace Hansen

Design Contributors: Laura Rask, Dorothy Toth

Library of Congress Control Number: 2015941983

Cataloging-in-Publication Data

Hansen, Grace.

Angel sharks / Grace Hansen.

p. cm. -- (Sharks)

ISBN 978-1-68080-149-1 (lib. bdg.)

Includes index.

1. Angel shark--Juvenile literature. I. Title.

597.3--dc23

2015941983

Table of Contents

Angel Sharks

Angel sharks live

in oceans. They like

warm and shallow water.

4

5

Angel sharks do not look like other sharks. They look more like stingrays. Their bodies are long and flat.

7

Their pectoral fins are **broad**. Their tails look the same as other shark tails.

8

9

Angel sharks can be brown. They can be reddish or gray, too. They have light and dark **markings** on their bodies.

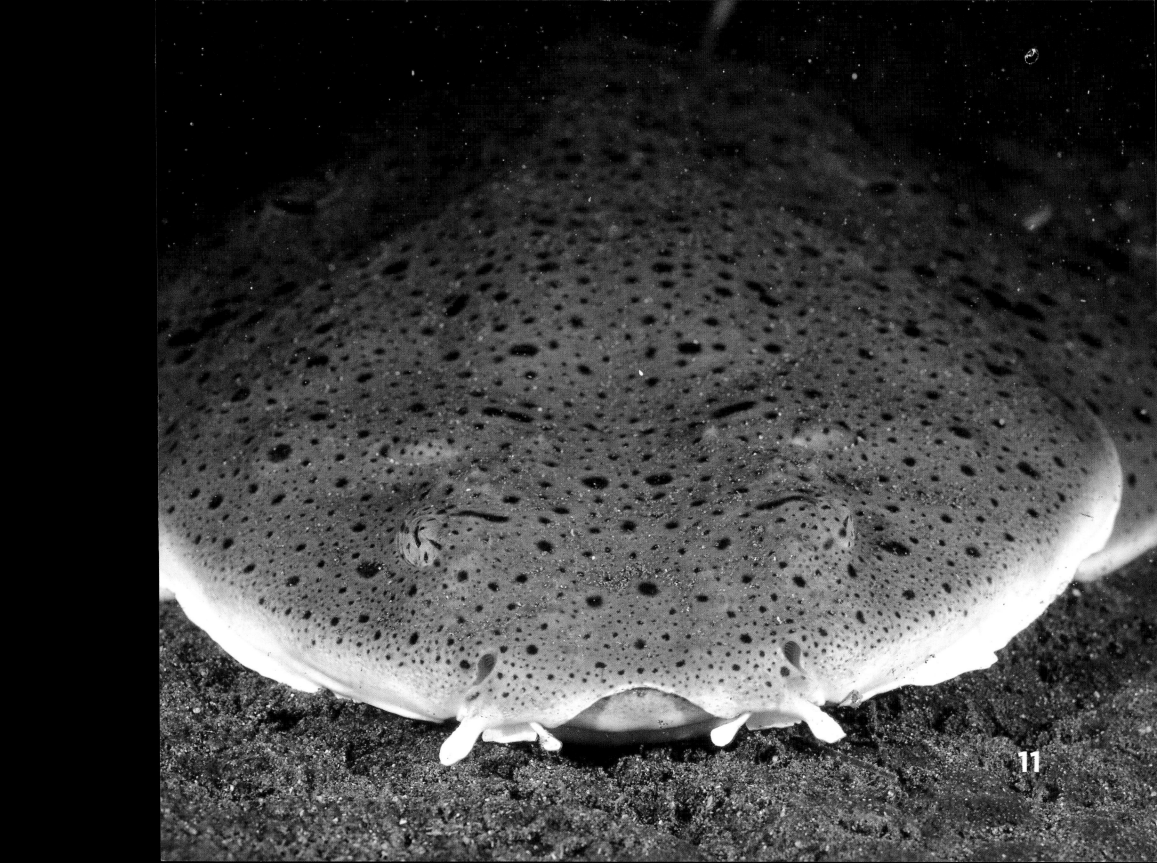

Food & Hunting

Angel sharks are

bottom-dwellers. They hide

in the sand. They wait for prey.

When prey swim by, angel sharks lunge. They trap prey with their strong jaws and sharp teeth.

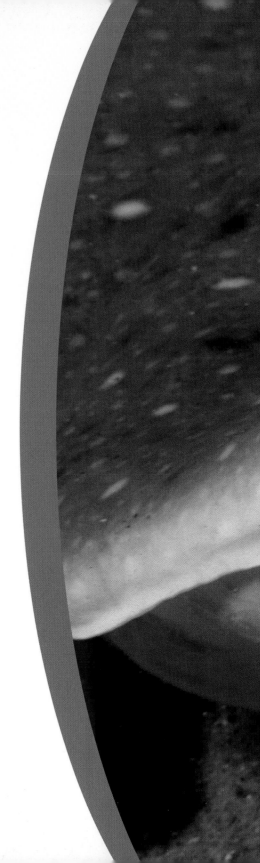

15

Angel sharks eat many kinds of fish. They also like squid and octopus. They eat other animals, too.

16

squid

octopus

17

Baby Angel Sharks

Baby sharks are called

pups. Angel sharks give

birth to around 10 pups.

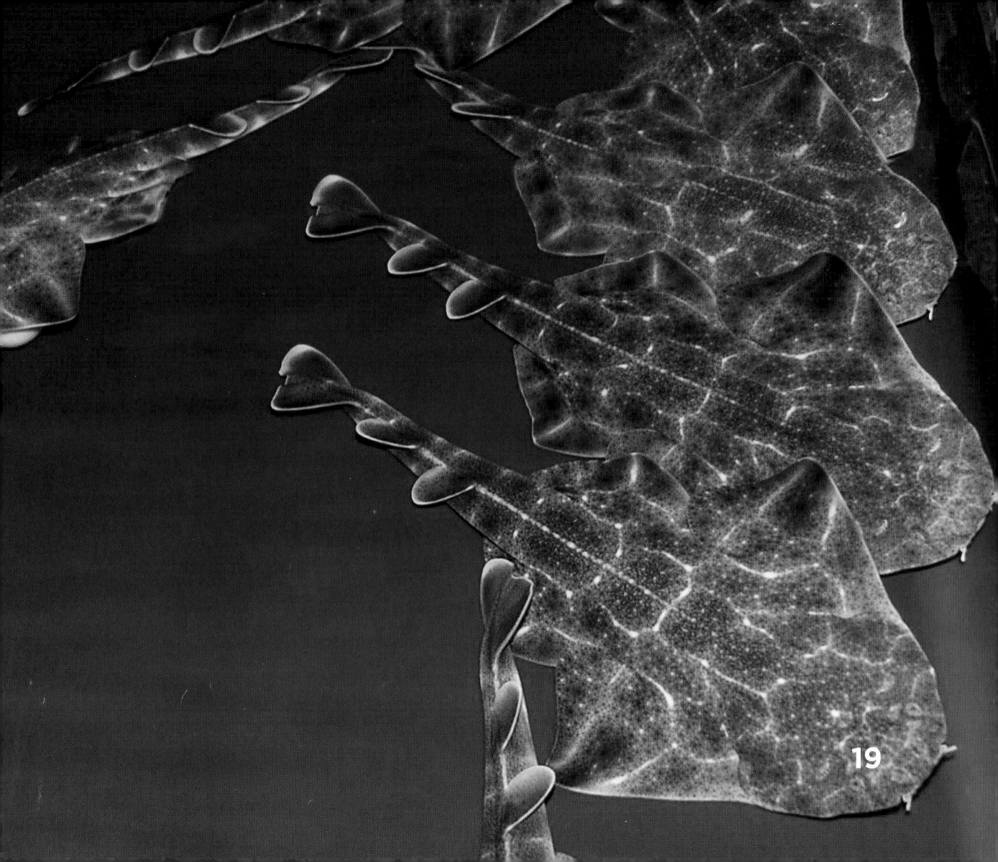

After birth, **pups** are on their own. They are about 9 inches (23 cm) long. They will grow to around 60 inches (152 cm).

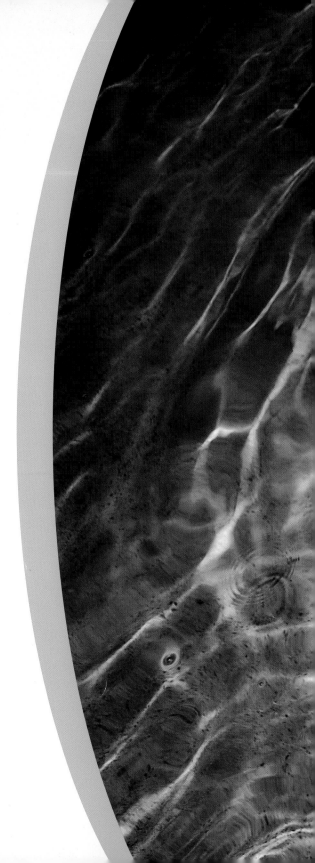

More Facts

- The Japanese angel shark is the largest angel shark species. It can grow up to 6.5 feet long (2 meters).

- Angel sharks breathe differently from other sharks. Most sharks need to move to breathe. Angel sharks do not.

- Angel sharks can live more than 30 years in the wild.

Glossary

bottom-dweller – a fish that lives and feeds on a river, lake, or ocean floor.

broad – wide from side to side.

markings – a mark or pattern of marks on an animal's fur, feathers, or skin.

pup – a newborn animal.

Index

abdokids.com

Use this code to log on to abdokids.com and access crafts, games, videos, and more!

Abdo Kids Code:
SAK1491